COMPLICATED
CATS
A FIDDLY FELINE COLORING BOOK

THIS BOOK BELONGS TO

....

ILLUSTRATED BY
ANTONY BRIGGS

COMPLICATED
COLORING
www.complicatedcoloring.com

FIRST EDITION

PUBLISHED BY COMPLICATED COLORING

WWW.COMPLICATEDCOLORING.COM

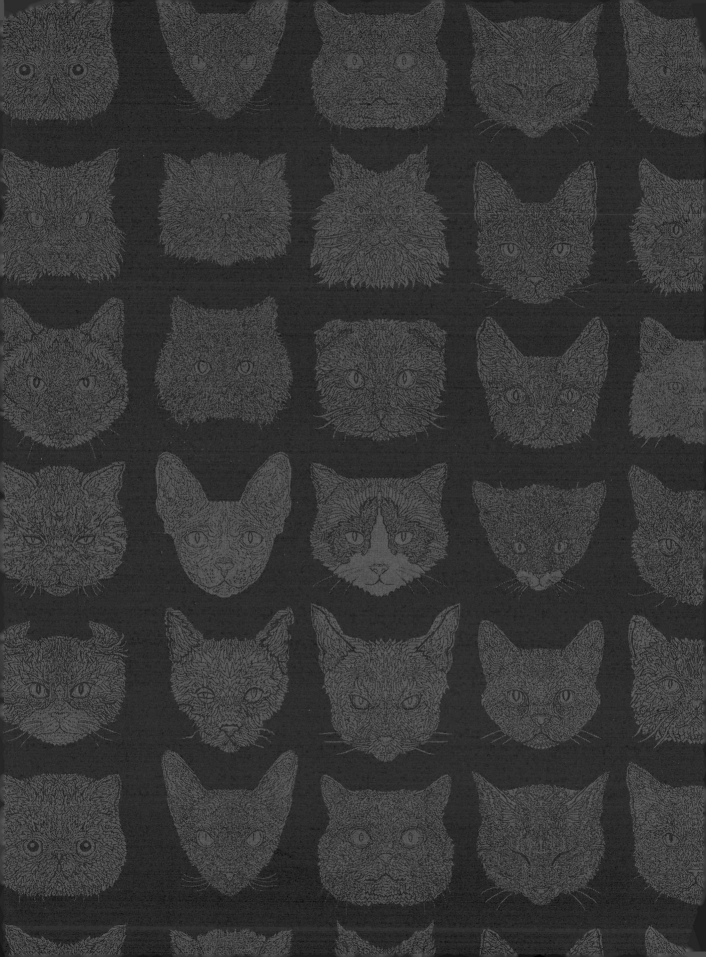

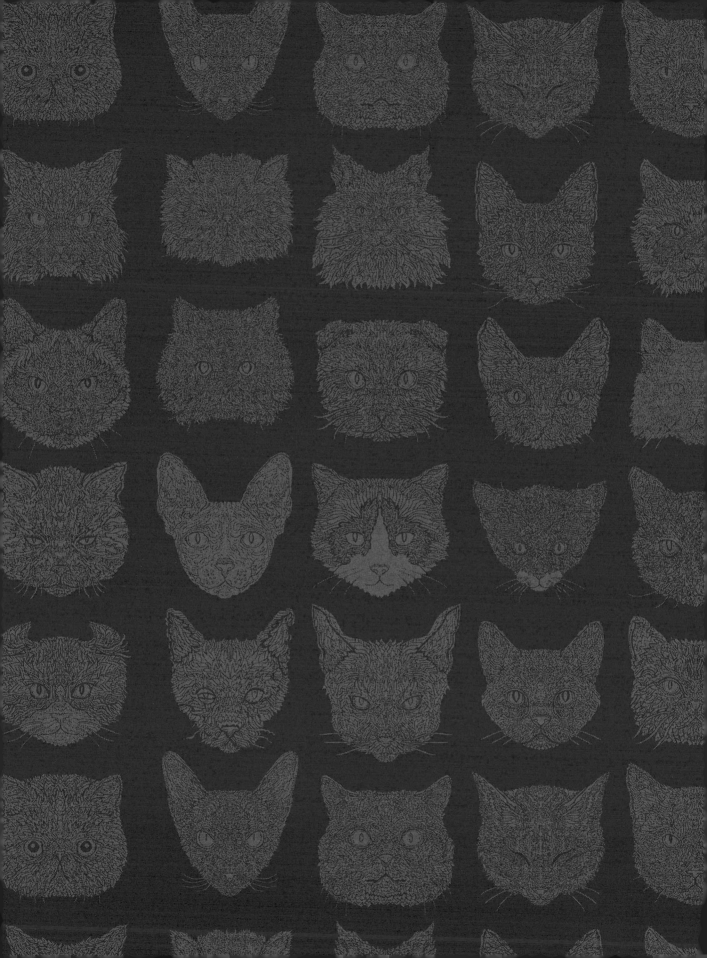

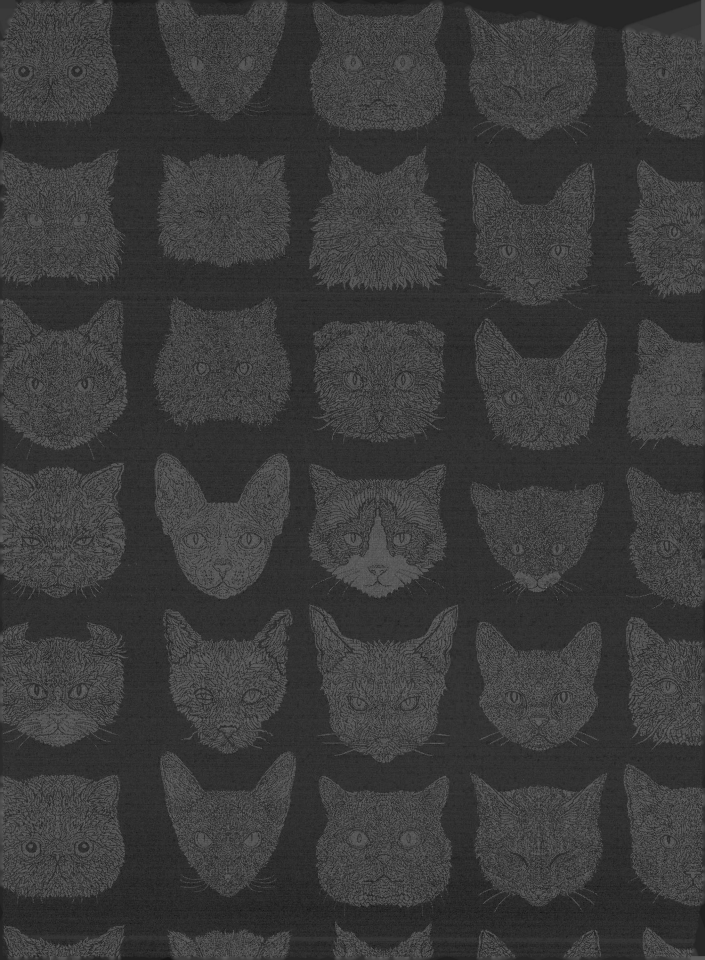

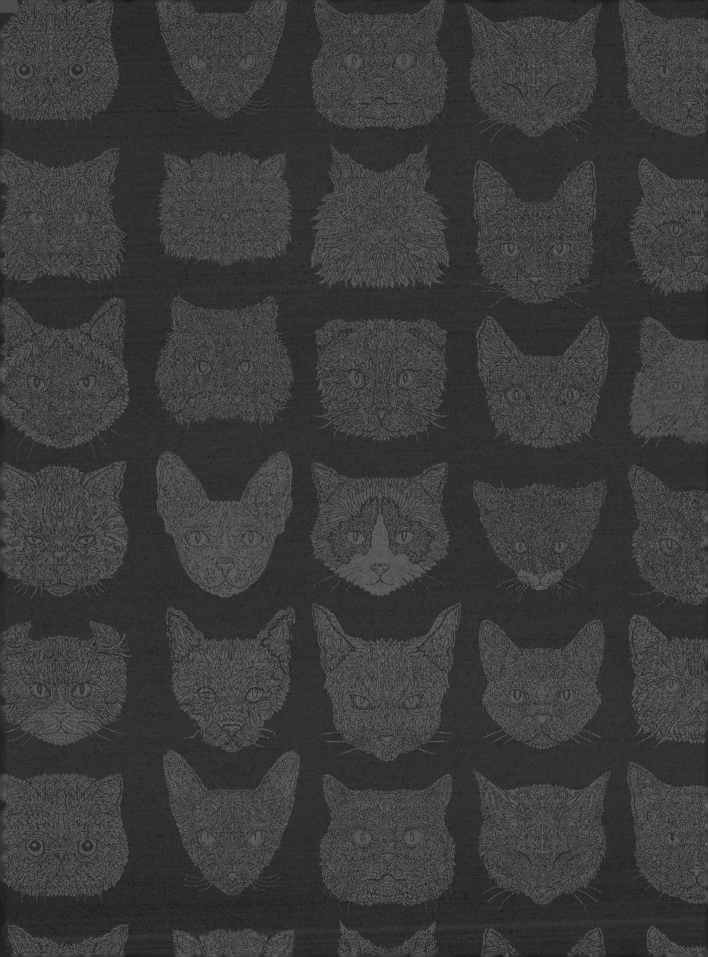

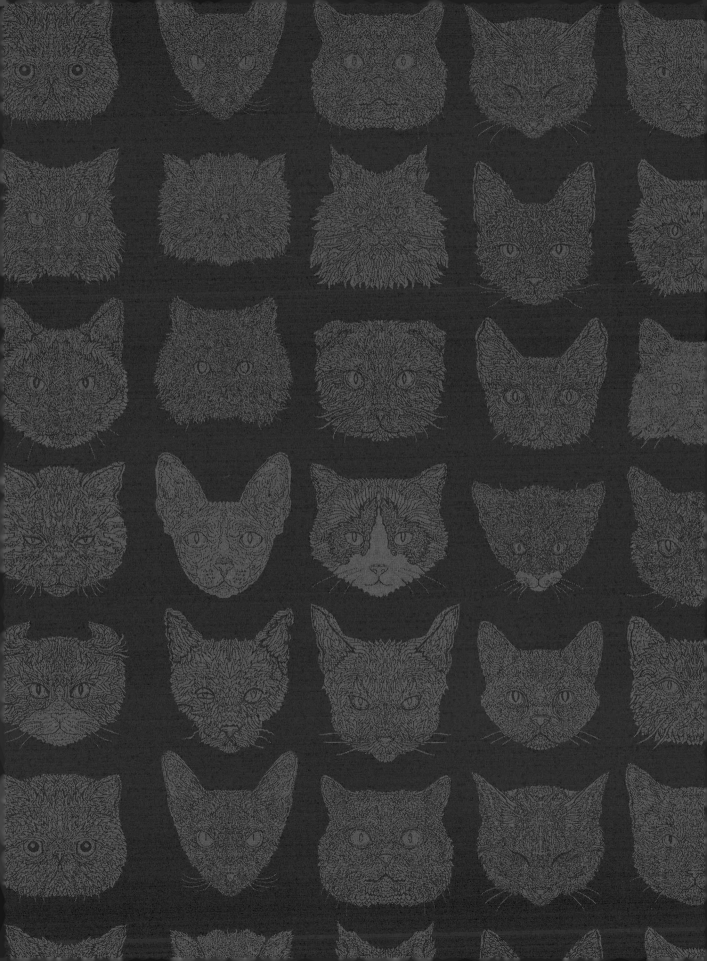

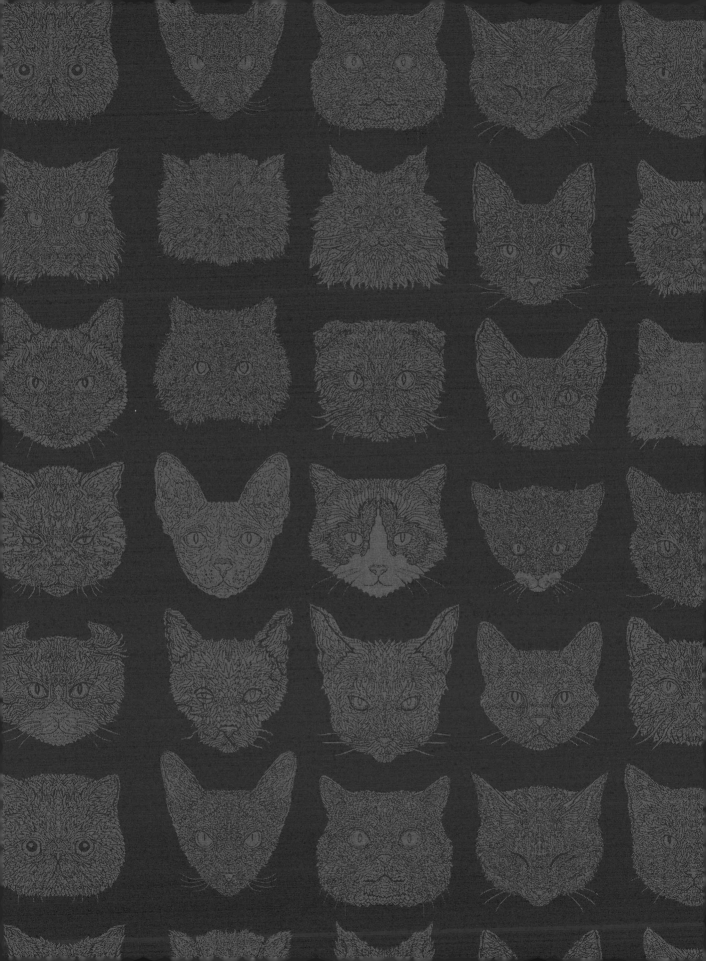

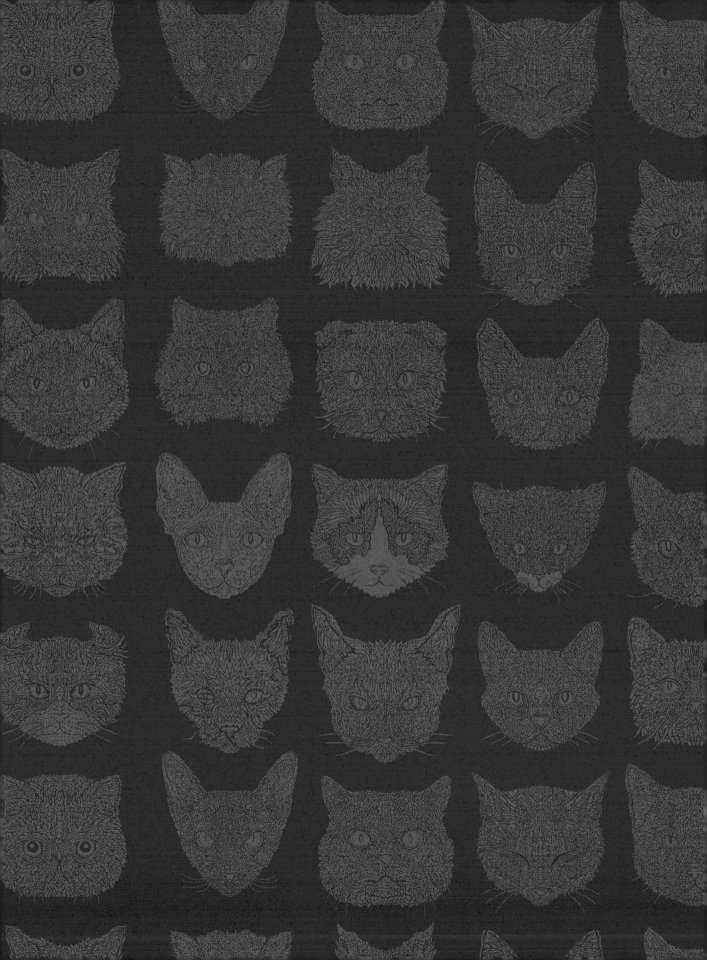

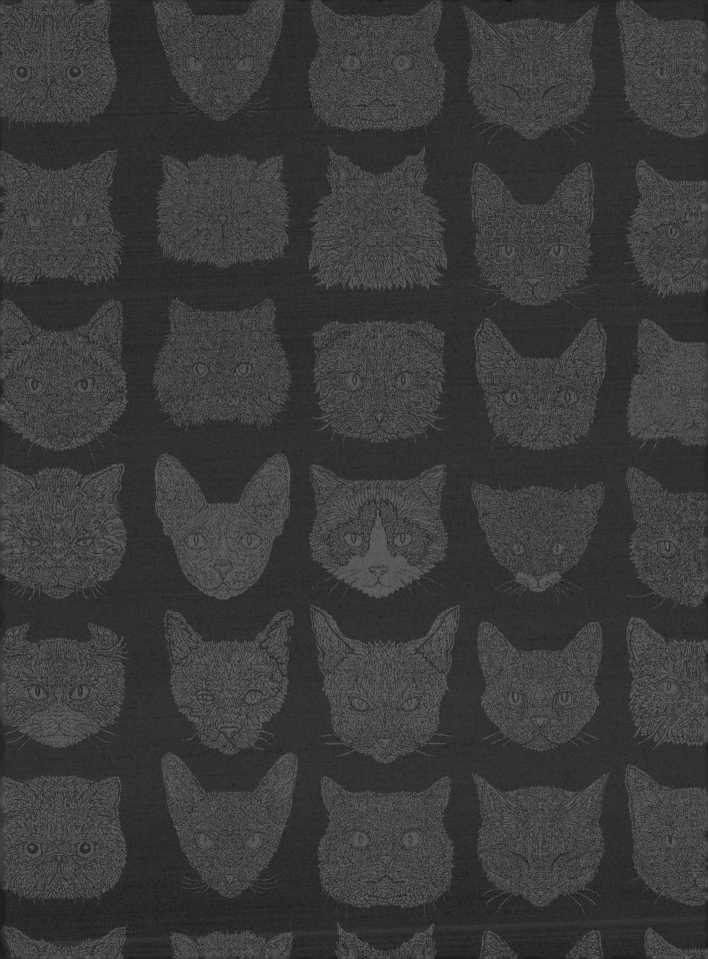

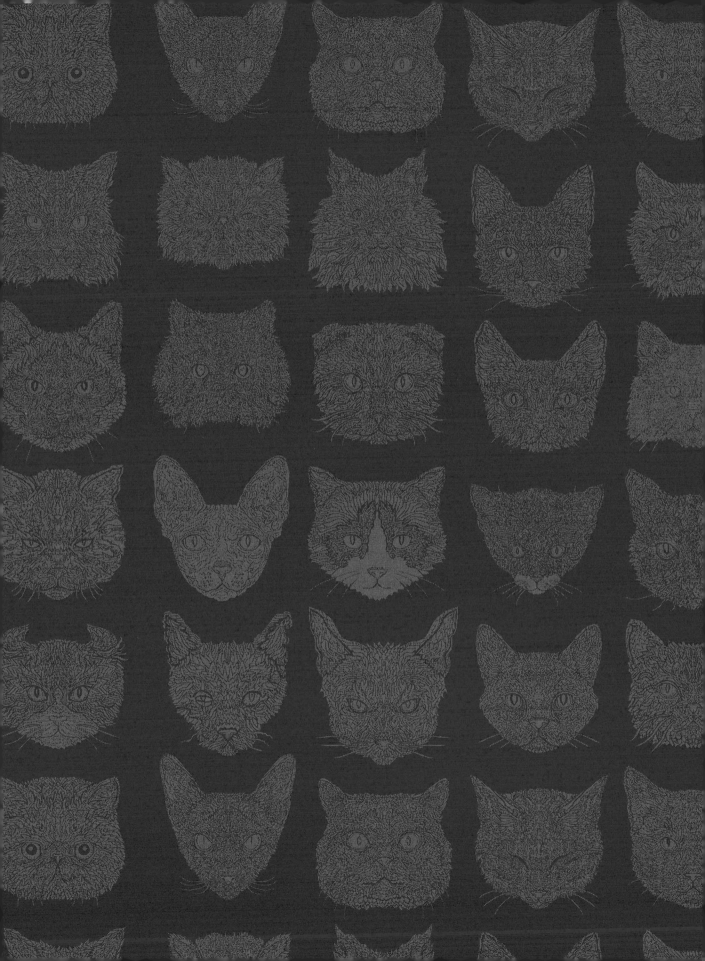

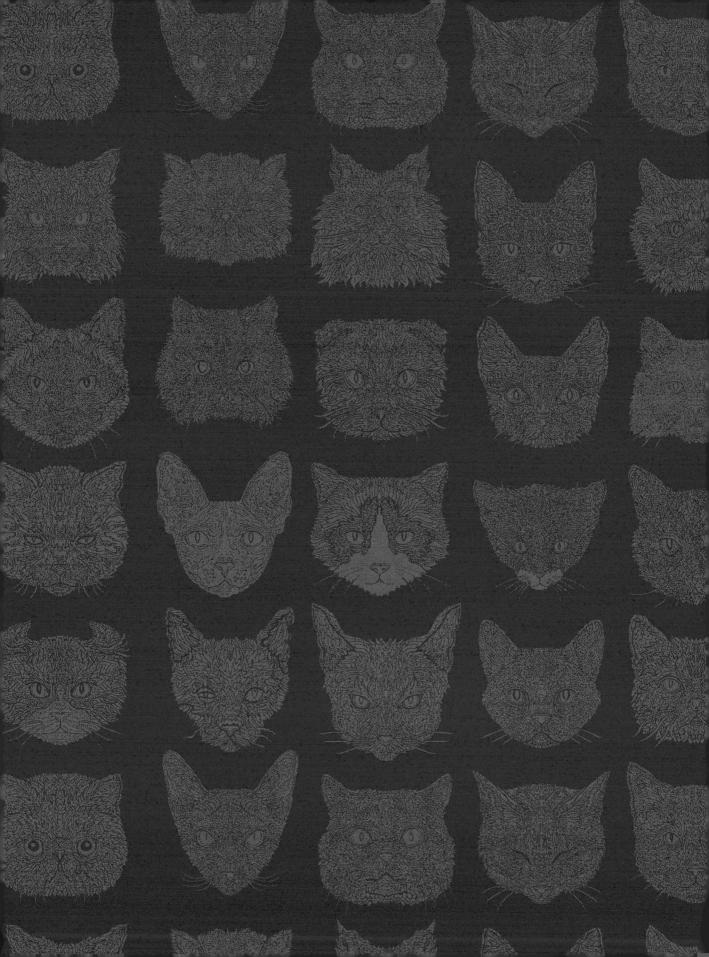

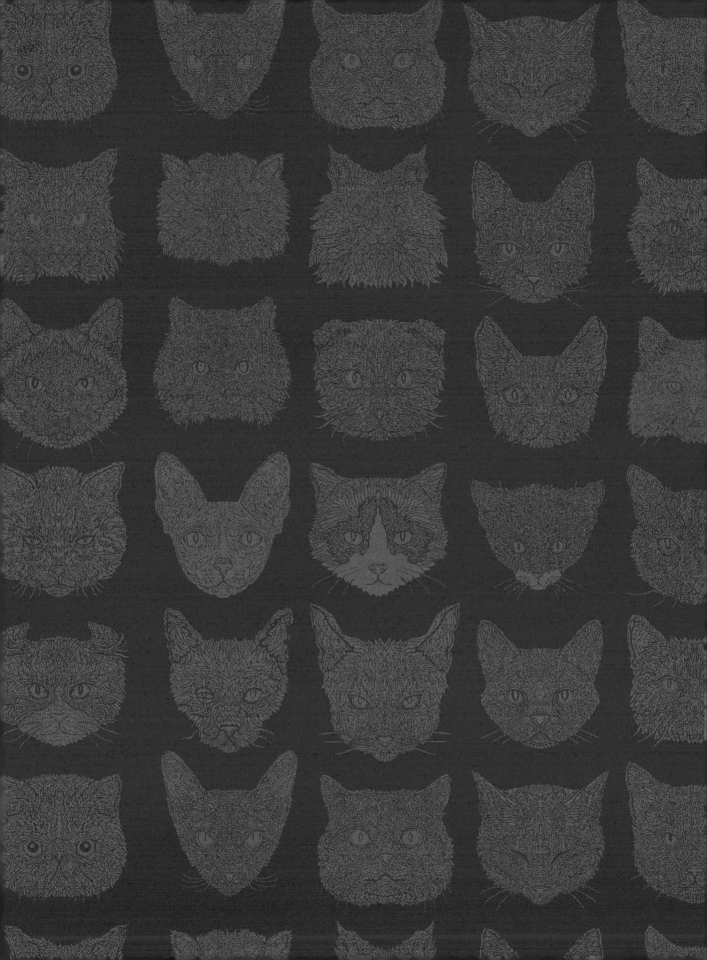

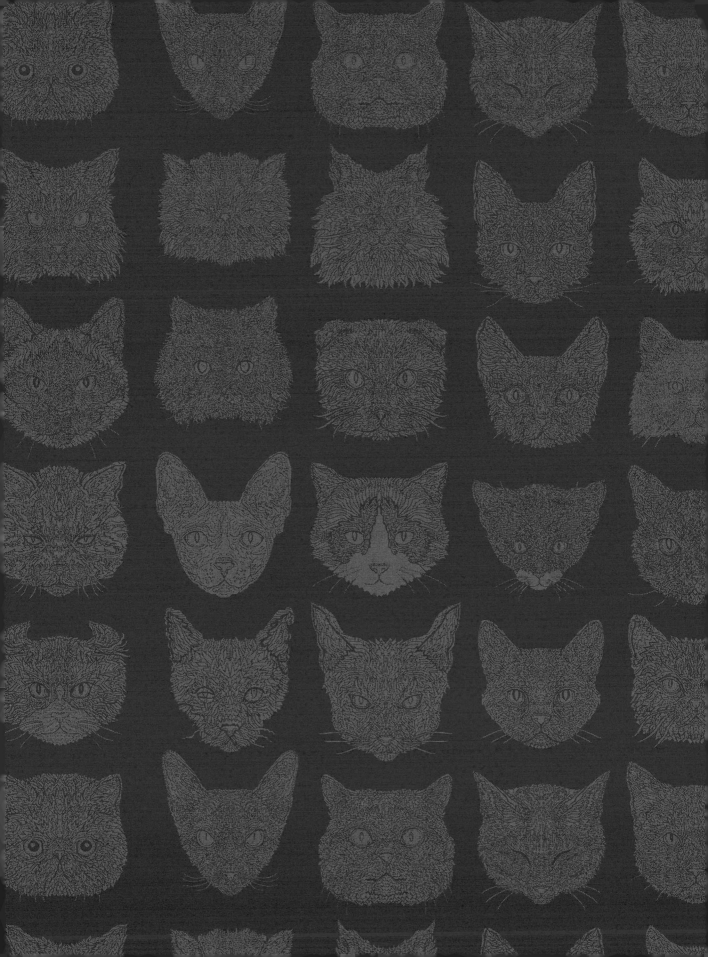

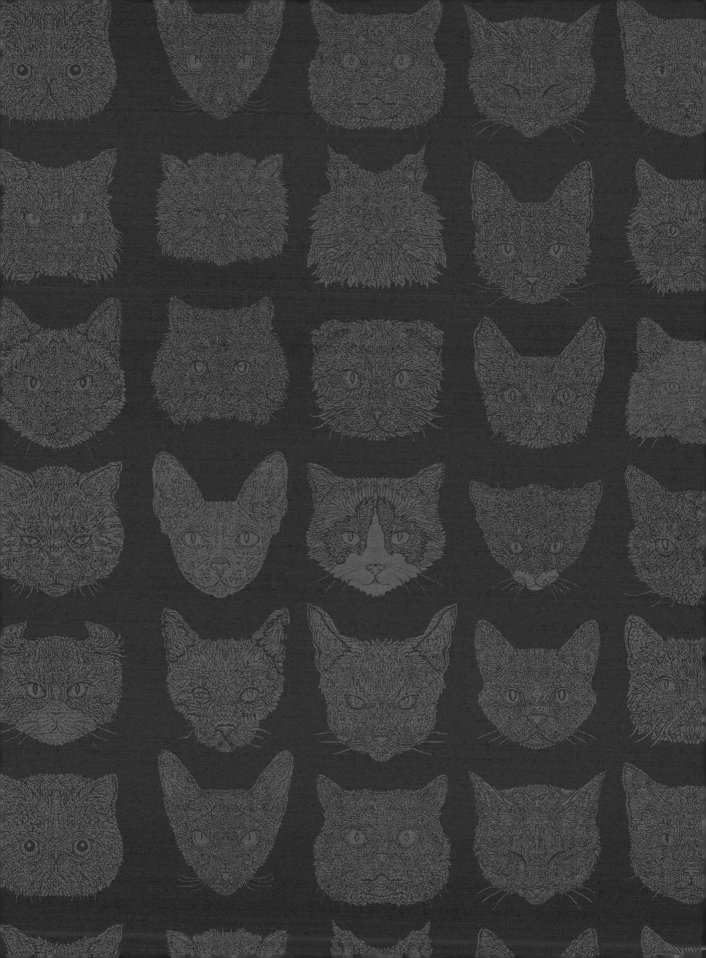

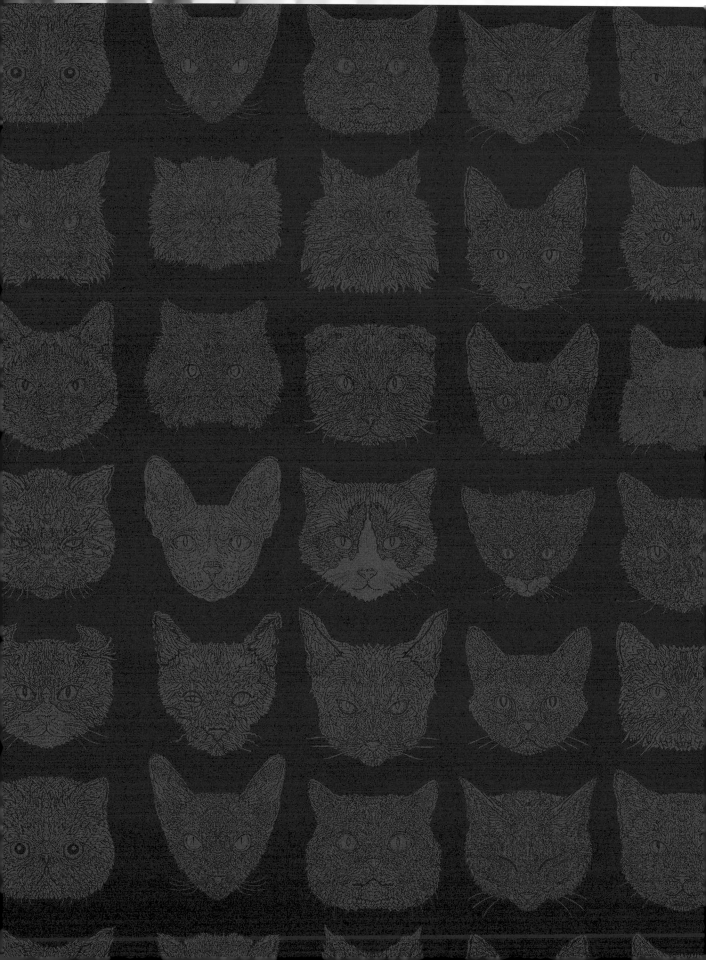

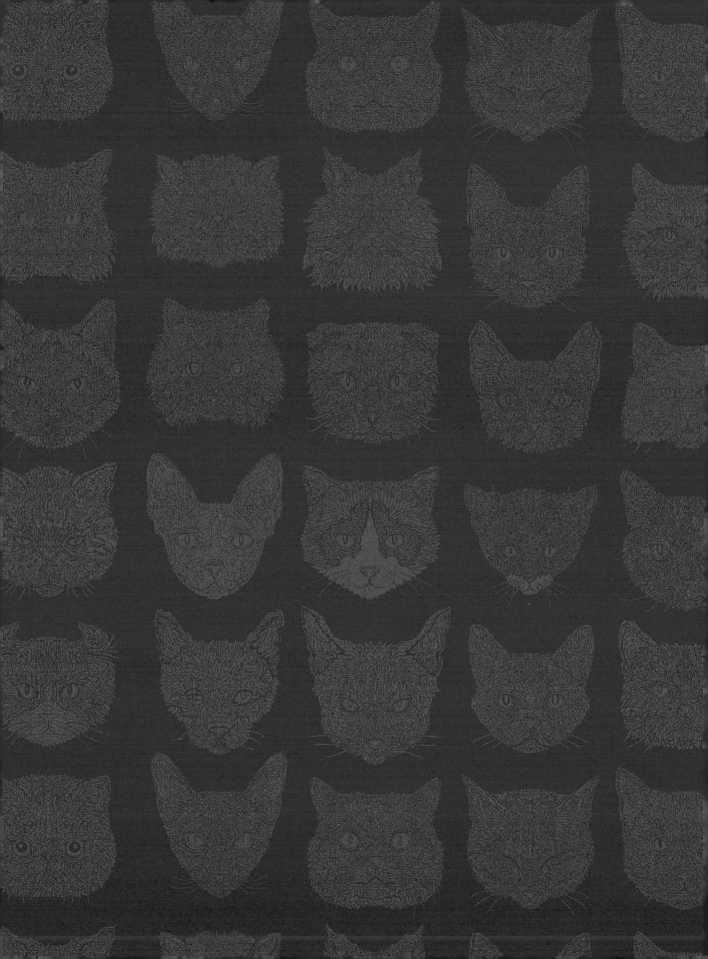

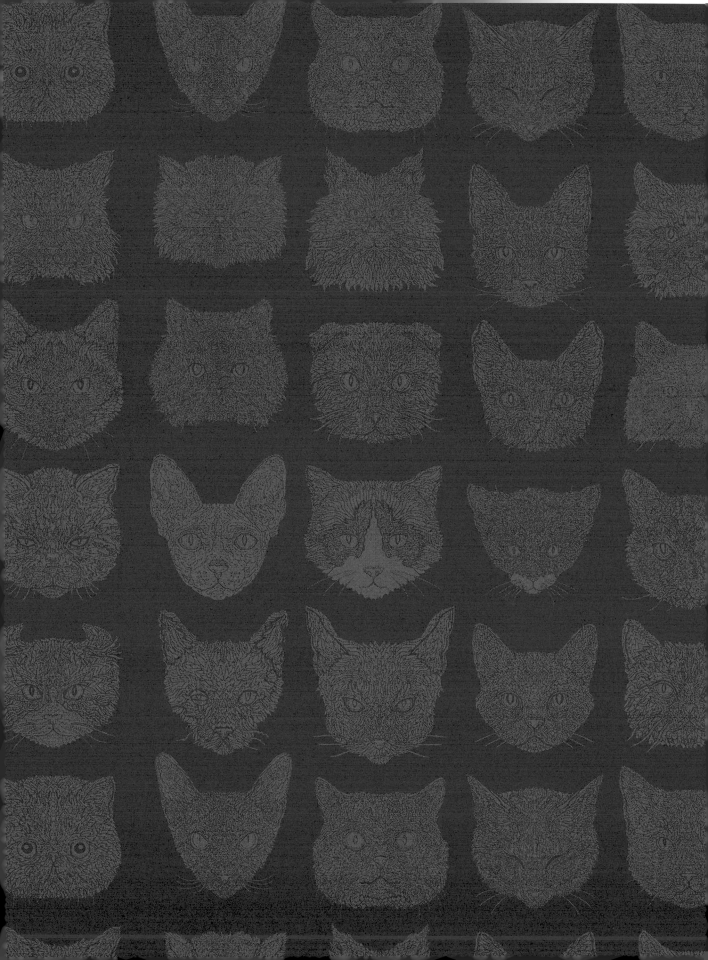

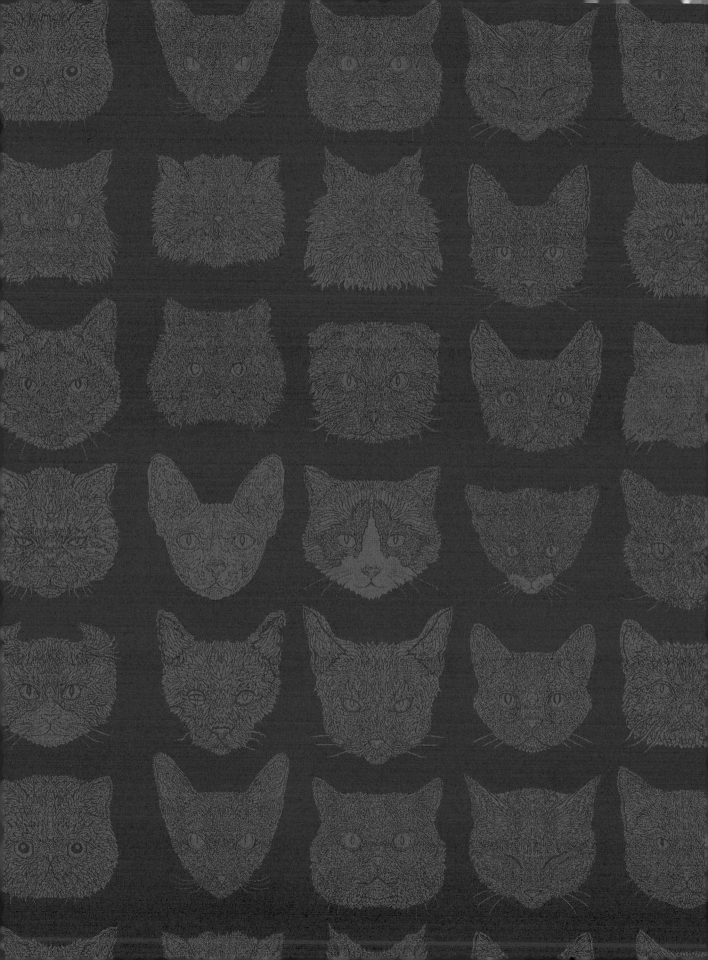

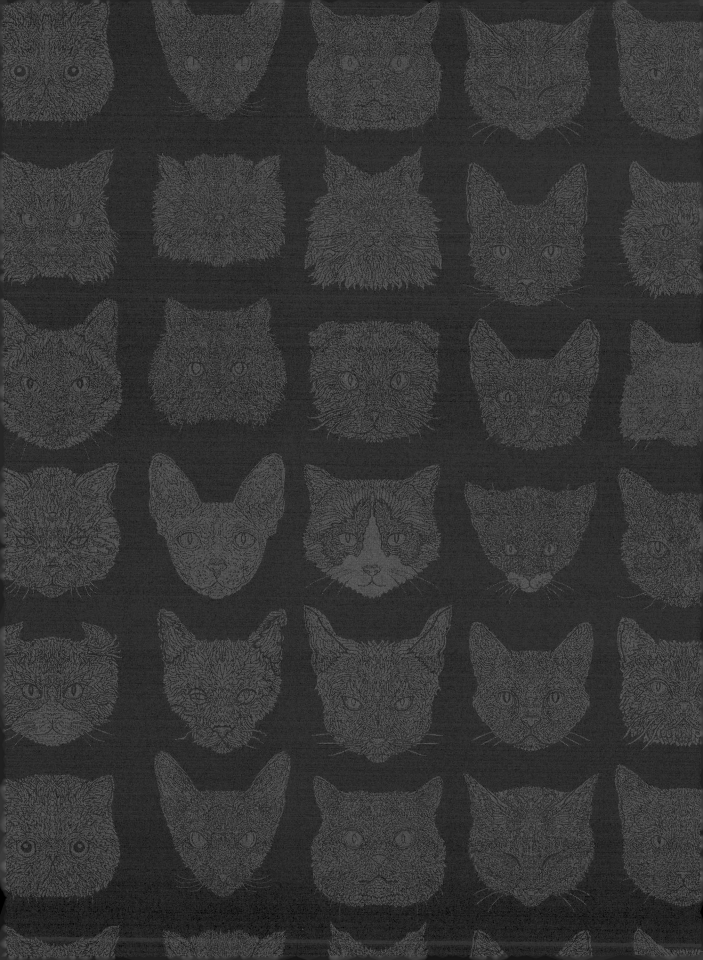

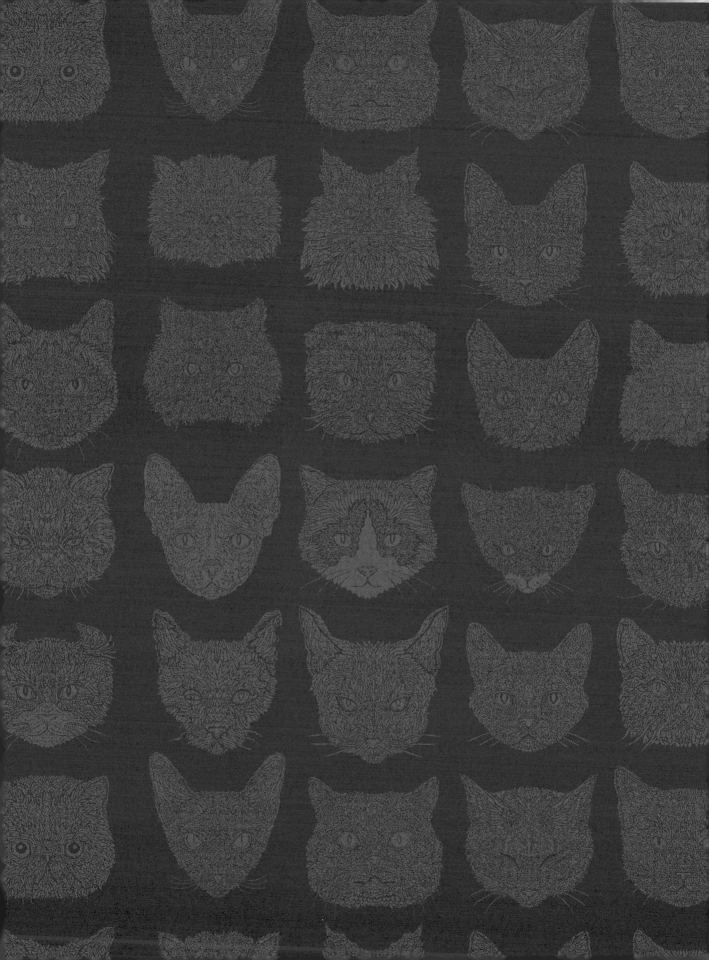

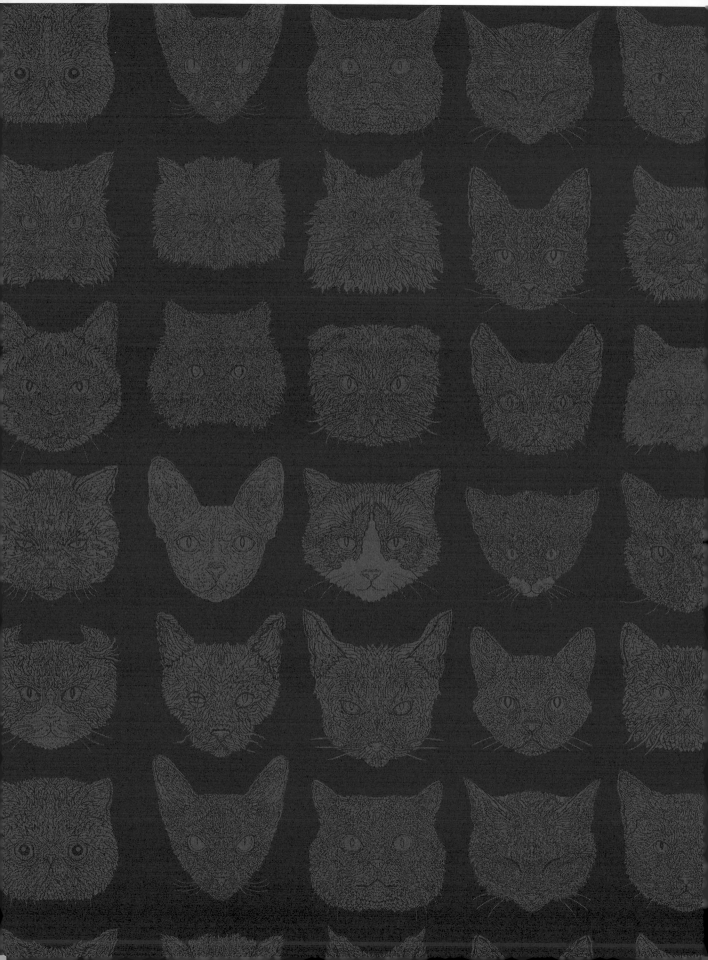

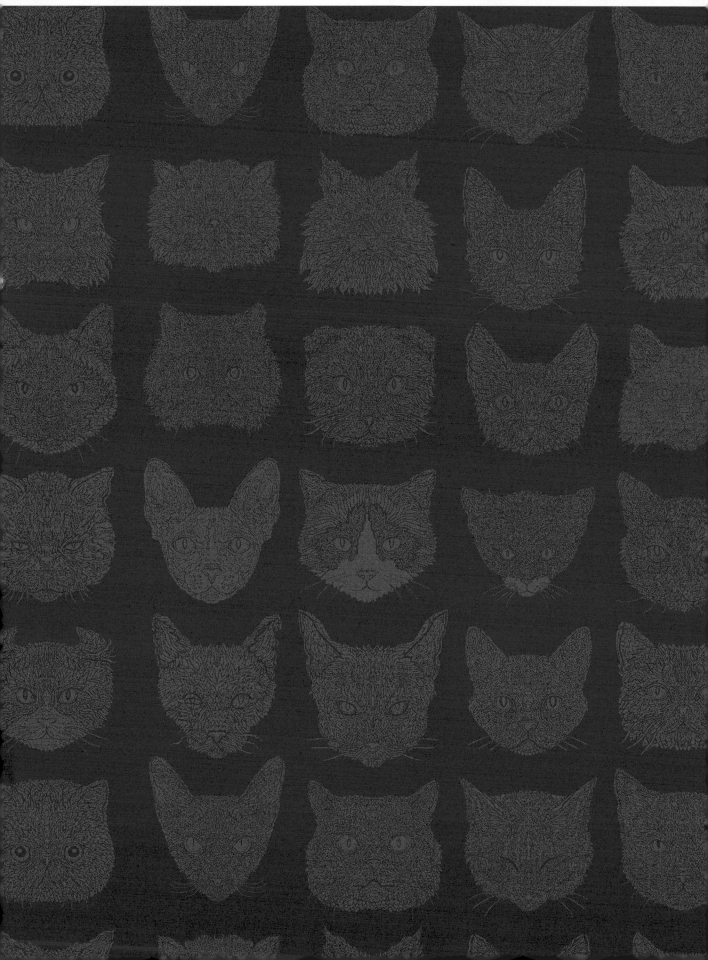

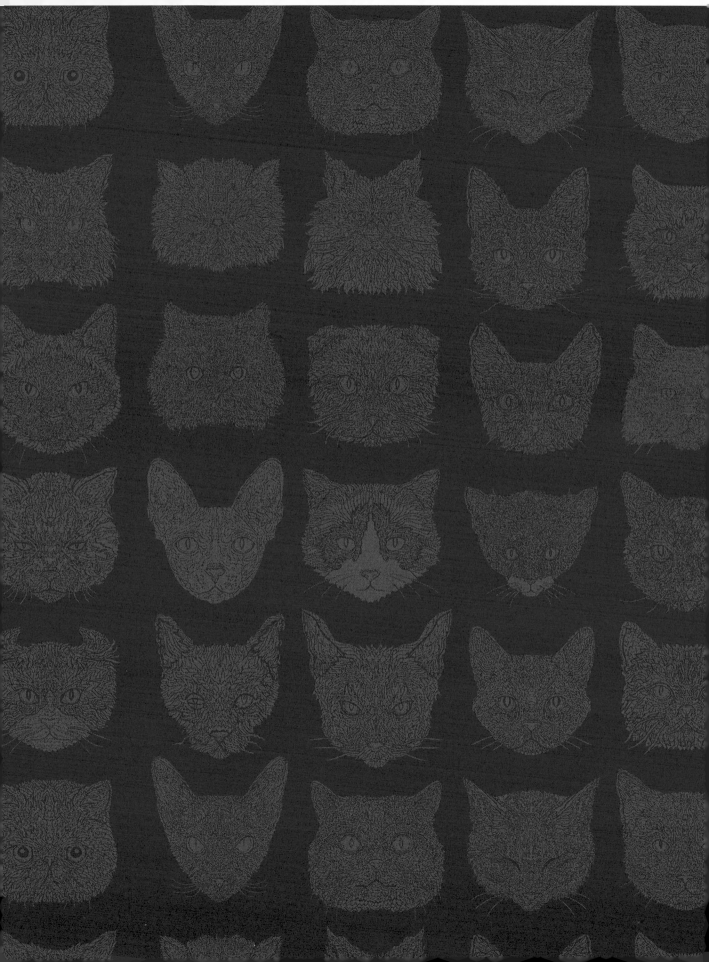

OTHER BOOKS IN THIS SERIES:

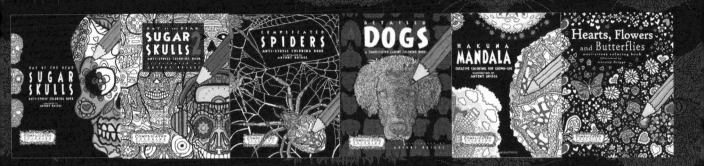

WE LOVE TO SEE YOUR COMPLETED, COMPLICATED MASTERPIECES

SHARE YOUR WORK ONLINE AT:

f FACEBOOK.COM/COLORING.BOOKS.FOR.GROWN.UPS/

OR

O @COMPLICATEDCOLORING

YOU CAN ALSO VISIT OUR WEBSITE:

WWW.COMPLICATEDCOLORING.COM

FOR UP-TO-DATE NEWS AND FREE PRINTABLE PAGES.

IF YOU HAVE ENJOYED THIS BOOK,
PLEASE LEAVE A REVIEW.

THANKS

Printed by Amazon Italia Logistica S.r.l.
Torrazza Piemonte (TO), Italy

16470814R00062